The Gasconade Review Presents:
39 Feet High and Rising

Edited by
John Dorsey and Jason Ryberg

Spartan Press
Kansas City, Missouri
spartanpresskc.com

OAC Books
89 Eagle Lane
Belle, MO, 65013

Copyright © 2017
Edited by John Dorsey, Jason Ryberg
First Edition 1 3 5 7 9 10 8 6 4 2
ISBN: 978-1-946642-31-8
LCCN: 2017955533

Design, edits and layout: Jason Ryberg, John Dorsey
Cover and interior photos of the 2017 flood: Jacob Warden, courtesy of The Maries County Advocate

All rights reserved. No part of this publication may be reproduced or transmitted in any form or by any means, electronic or mechanical, including photocopying, recording or by info retrieval system, without prior written permission from the author.

The Gasconade Review is a literary and arts journal, focusing exclusively on Missouri poets, writers and artists, that appears twice a year.

When I was appointed the first Poet Laureate of Belle, MO at the end of 2016, my first order of business, in addition to having community readings, was to create a literary publication that the city could call its own, you are now holding the first volume of that journal in your hands. After I moved to Missouri one of first things I began to notice immediately is that our region had poets coming out of woodwork from every direction and in every community, the end result here is a testament to our love of words.

A special thanks must be given to Mayor Steve Vogt, Barbara Huse, the Friends of the Belle Library, Jason Ryberg, Osage Arts Community—Mark McClane and Tony Hayden.

—John Dorsey, Founder and Co-Editor,
Gasconade Review

CONTENTS

Above and Below by Greg Edmondson

STEVEN H. BRIDGENS
Gravy on the Taters / 1
Rural Drama / 2
cicadas interrupted / 4

RAPHAEL MAURICE
[Rectitude] / 6
[Gas Station in Gerald] 7
[My Better Life in the Country] / 8

JASON RYBERG
Sometimes the Moon
 Is Nothing More Than the Moon / 10
What Else To Do? / 13
Treehouse Fallen
 in the Backwoods / 15

Field by Justin Hamm / 17

DANIEL CROCKER
I Don't Write Political Poems / 18
Elmo Goes Emo / 21
Sestina McRib / 22

BRETT UNDERWOOD
How Far Does the Head Turn? / 24
Day / 27
Slick / 29

JORDI ALONSO
[p. 42] / 31
[p. 88] / 32
[pp. 228-229] / 33

JEANETTE POWERS
Throw Yourself Down the Hill / 34

VICTOR CLEVENGER
a poem about a woman i never got to know / 43
we stand next to a river / 45
when / 46

KEVIN W. PEERY
Rosie / 47
Cecil / 49
Shaver / 50

Photos of the Great Flood of 2017 by Jacob Warden / 52

CHIGGER MATTHEWS
Working On My Car / 58
Optimism and Confidence / 59
Memory / 60

HUNTER PENDER
I Could Write You into a Soft Evening / 61
Did it Hurt? / 63
Write Me on Waves / 65

JIM MCGOWIN
Unum / 66
Antigone / 70
Sigma Octanis / 72

Nobody Lives Here Anymore by Justin Hamm / 74

JOHN DORSEY
Nikki, Full of Grace / 75
The Midwestern Guide to Time Travel / 77
Moon Over Eufaula, Oklahoma / 78

JUSTIN HAMM
Arthur and Marie, 1961 / 79
First Lesson in Vietnam / 81
Pay Phones in the Underworld / 82

WILLIAM TROWBRIDGE
To the Cialis Lovers / 84
Head Out on the Highway / 85
The Crazy Lady / 86

Spinner by Greg Edmondson / 88

Author bios / 89

STEVE VOGT
Brock / 96

Butterfly and Fist by Jason Ryberg

This book is dedicated to the memory
of Brock Andrew Vogt,
January 4, 1984 — October 31, 2016.

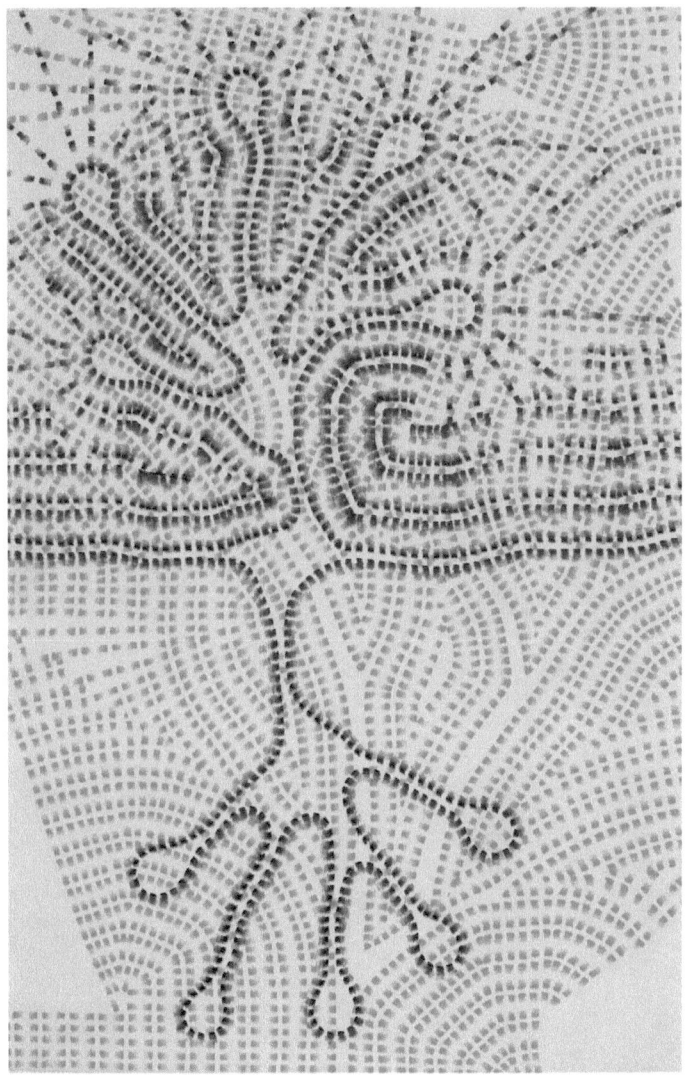

"Above and Below (Horizon Line)," Greg Edmondson, pencil on paper, mylar and collage

STEVEN H. BRIDGENS

Gravy on the Taters

Every day since my wreck has just been more gravy
on the taters.

We'll all be gone a long, long time or so I've been told.
Not much to worry about there.

Some days I care a lot about that but not that many,
really, anymore.

I pretty much just want to go out to breakfast,
drink up a bunch of really good coffee and see a matinee.

Some days though I get all fired up about not-that-much
or whose- whom but now I'm really trying to put more
space between them and theirs.

I need to get outdoors more, walk in the woods,
look for lichens and fungus growing on tree branches
for my collection but until then
I'll just try to take it easy—

naptime, you know.

Rural Drama

Poison ivy grows thickly on one side of my broken stoop,
several gruesome thorny cacti on the other—
my own Scylla and Charybdis.

A huge thicket of thorny roses reaches out to cover the house,
blocking my door. The grass needs cutting desperately
and suckers are coming up everywhere.

A lonely Red Hawk flies directly overhead, stationary
in the afternoon breeze—look out below! Our tabby cat
is hunting in the field just outside the back door, always
on the lookout for birds and bunnies, relishing both.

My black coffee almost reflects the cloudless sky—
super Buddha-mind blue today, washed so clean
by the mighty rains we've had all week up here,
way North of the river, far from the calamities of the city.

The people there leave me alone now, more or less.
Their drama seems only like distant bells whose echo
just doesn't seem to reach across the brown and flooded moat.

Our rural drama here amounts to, at most, a wasp or a rooster
getting into the house and wandering about unescorted
or perhaps a possum family rustling about under the house.

The big tractor mows on, cutting only the widest swaths
of our acreage, as if to say—Don't sweat the small stuff.

I've big plans for those roses but they will wait, won't they?

Further comments have been filed with the Tibetan Embassy
just down the road. We patiently await the Ambassador's
laugh and answering wave.

cicadas interrupted

the storm builds slowly, sprinkling droplets gently
from clouds towering behind my trees

thunder shatters the distance, silencing the cicadas
singing in the grass

the storm can be clearly seen from each window,
out there just over the silver barn on the hill

the dusty windows are covered with thorny vines—
some have broken into the house between the glass panes
and their old wood frames, seeking any possible way in,
perhaps a reminder to persevere, somehow

church bells across the way annunciate the passage
of summer—one bell at the quarter hour,
two bells at the half, then three bells, then four

cars race by, their sound far away in the distance,
is only a whoosh of white noise, just like the real world

the thunder rattles and booms, shaking the windows
and my dishes in their drying rack

big and little lightning flashes tease us—pink, red, gold,
all traveling along with the massive wall of grey clouds
rolling our way

darkness finally falls with the rain, now heavy as it soaks
everything

a pair of beautiful red and black butterflies sneaks right
in through the open kitchen door, seeking sanctuary

and, of course, they immediately seek out the half-closed,
vine-covered window and are now trapped there

throwing themselves furiously against the dusty glass,
time and time again, seeking only to escape
their new found refuge,

then right on cue, an ambulance races up the hill,
mercifully speeding our way, coming to help, I assume

the rain finally dribbles to a stop and the cicadas pick up
just where they left off, having never missed a beat

RAPHAEL MAURICE

[Rectitude]

   The police caught me near these weeping willows
creeping up lakeside. I gave up under dawn's
wrack and ribbon. They took what little I had.

And I was long gone, babbling my season's luck
and miscarriages.
The county jail. Silent as a brick, stiller than God.

I crashed out on the bunks logic, its rectitude. *Rectitude.*
What a strange word for dead monks to thrash about.

And I dreamed the horse-faced sheriff was reading
from a sacred book. His boots propped on the desk.
His words scattered by an oscillating fan.

      It was litany. It was the liturgy at my father's funeral,
reverent as the edge of morning glories, a reckoning.

It was a catalogue of tender girls I'd loved,
their terrible fates blowing against those crooked trees.

[Gas Station in Gerald]

Yesterday, my father saw me for the first time.
We were in his Impala, and my hands were fumbling
for a cigarette.

Here, he said. *Take the money.*
His eyes were broken, twisted, the way lightning is
against the open dead skies of Gerald, Missouri.

I can't. I just can't

I don't know why we had stopped, but we had.
I remembered the pencil box he'd bought me
on my first day at school.
Thinking of it—the color of old blood,
the wood worn smooth—thinking of it,
I want to bring him closer to me.

My God. Those years in the ward, he said
in Gerald, Missouri.
My God.

[My Better Life in the Country]

I suppose I should tell of the things I liked here.
I liked the way hay bales looked like giant, golden tablets,
and often I thought God would appear and reach down,
take a pill and then drink from a water-swollen lake.

Horses. Just out the window, the fields of wheat stirring against
their great bodies, and if you approached with carrots or apples,
you would know love and fear. You would understand, though
you had not yet read of Hippolytus drowning in magnetic surf,
your own desire to be near horses.

I would take sticks and make crosses, taping the pieces together.
And through the fields, I heard hymns and songs, as I curled
like a violin-scroll beneath a tree. I would awake,
crosses at my feet, after a good sleep beneath an oak.

I liked the way my mother, who smelled of fresh laundry,
hung clothes on the line my father put up. I even like to recall
them bickering. She had instructed him on how to hang
the cord and where to place the poles. And he, in his wry,
southern voice: *Opinions are inexpensive, dear.*

I liked him reading from Homer at night. I liked the way
the sea, which was simply the field with its horses and hay bales,
roared and hushed me to sleep. I would drift off with the Iliad
beneath my pillow, muttering, *father, father.*

And though it burns at times, I don't exactly regret that later
I would go mad with what he had taught me: Greek letters
on wax paper hung like ghosts from the dormitory walls.
I saw Alpha to Omega borne into buildings that galloped at me.
Useless when a doctor muttered back, *ten-year recovery.*

Most of all, I liked the possibility of forgiveness. I like it now.
And I have always liked the way memories have an order
all their own— like a boy arranging lettered blocks
upon the steps of his parents' home, or a mare nudging a colt,
guided by a logic that we can only witness.

JASON RYBERG

Sometimes the Moon Is Nothing More Than the Moon

Sometimes the moon comes down
(if she happens to be in town)
from her royal couch of clouds
to drink with us (my shadow
and me) when no one else will.

Sometimes the moon rings
like a temple bell on a cold night,
signaling the beginning (or end)
of something important and radiates
with a halo of steam like a luminous
ball of dry ice.

Sometimes the moon is a curved dagger
that some Bedouin bandit prince
might have carried in the blue and grainy
late, late show of my childhood dreams.

Sometimes the moon is a white rose
that drunken fools inevitably try
to shoot arrows and poems at,
knowing full-well that both return
to Earth with potentially dangerous results.

Sometimes the moon is a pallid face
peering in at us through a Winter window
scene while the radio begins to glow
with a moody Ellington Indigo
and a car down on the street is struggling
to clear the early frost from its throat.

Sometimes the moon is a cop's
flashlight cutting a cautious path
through film-noir ghosts of gutter steam.

Sometimes the moon is a 60-watt bulb
shining from the back porch,
out into the sweaty, firefly-choked,
backyard jungle nights of long ago.

Sometimes the moon is a guard tower spot,
always trying to catch us with its magic circle
whenever we make our midnight raids, over the walls,
into the Garden of Earthly Delights.

Sometimes the moon is a silver dollar
that's been sheared in two by a dull
and rusty pair of tin snips.

Sometimes the moon is a shiny dime
flattened on a railroad track,
in which, if one looks just right,
a semblance of Roosevelt's confident
and reassuring smirk can still be seen.

Sometimes the moon is a fat, blue
androgynous Buddha, grinning out
at the universe in every direction at once.

Sometimes the moon is a single bright eye
of a dark god of the ancient world,
peering down at us through a hole torn
in the top of a circus tent of clouds,
or up from an inversely alternate underworld
through the dimensional portal
of a swollen, marshy pond.

Sometimes the moon is nothing more
than the moon.

No.

That's never true.

What Else To Do?
with deepest apologies to the ghosts of Li Po, Tu Fu and Su Tung Po

Night, and the first few tentative drops
of a much-needed and long-prayed-for
summer rain going *plip, plip, plip*
down through the trees' many
cross-hatched layers of branches and leaves
to the summer-hot sidewalk below,

the trees like tattered beach umbrellas
sprouting, here and there, along the banks
of this lazy river of newly-laid tarmac,

a shy ghost in the attic window across the street,
tiny voices in the wind and grass
whispering choruses of praise (each to each)
to the Grand Schemata Of Peoples / Places / Things,
the micro-cosmic minutia of it all and all other
various originators of little and large moments
of deep enlightenment, in between.

And here I am (again, it seems),
legs in *faux* lotus postion, at the epicenter
of who knows how many known,
unknown and very possibly unknowable
spheres and ellipses of influence.

What else to do, then,
but raise my pint bottle up to the grinning,
blue Buddha moon to catch a view of him
through the brandy's amber luminescence
and the streaming, CinemaScopic projection
of clouds against the sky, and salute
his blissed-out, other-worldly magnificence?

My skeleton is an aching
abstract construct.

My heart is an old,
abandoned country church.

My mind is a flickering street light
at the heart of a feathery flurry
of poems that may never be finished.

Treehouse Fallen
in the Backwoods

Kind of a curious thing
to come upon a fallen treehouse,
all of a sudden, in the deep Missouri backwoods
(somewhere in that hazy, nebulous neutral zone
between North and South, noon and sundown);

one of those classic contemplative moments,
you might assume, that the universe
randomly puts in our paths, from time to time:

no other signs of civilization or human activity
of any kind for miles,

no reason one would even wildly speculate
that a person could stumble upon such a scene
in an otherwise still reasonably untouched
and primeval forest setting like this,

no hoary, haggard Old Man of the Mountains
or prancing Tom Bombadil-like character
to suddenly appear and tell us how
they've been here from the beginning,
how they've seen everything that's come
and gone in these parts since God was a baby,

no one who might have actually born witness
at that fateful moment of entropic dissolution
(in the endless, looping chain of fateful moments
that is this life of ours),

no one to answer what you could safely assume
would be the most obvious and pressing question
that would naturally come to one's mind
upon stumbling across a treehouse
fallen in the backwoods …

"Field," Justin Hamm

DANIEL CROCKER

I Don't Write Political Poems

We fed our kids
fish sticks
and we ate corn dogs
We knew it was poison

Sometimes we didn't eat

My mother fed me fat noodles
in watered-down tomato sauce
covered in spices from a plastic bottle

After three or four days
I imagined them worms
writhing in blood

In sixth grade
I had a cough for six months
but my only doctor trip
was for scabies

They itched in hard
red welts, living there
They were contagious
a poor people problem

My grandmother
read us the Bible at night instead
instead of what
no one ever said

I don't write political poems because
I'm no expert
on the economy or budgets
or cost cutting
measures

I *am* an expert
on being poor
of making a box of Kraft
Macaroni and Cheese stretch
like bloody fingers across a white
plate in a white apartment

There's some money now
and we give what we can
or so we say
but when I'm writing this
there's electricity, T.V,
an open can of Diet Coke
half-empty and flat
that I'll throw away

How many people
could I feed on what I
spend on Diet Coke

A number

Still others wait
while I wonder what
could have been done
with all the money
spent on beer
and whiskey
and cigarettes
all the cool poet tricks

Still others
hoard cash
in the name of Jesus
but it's hard to eat a tank
and bullets don't make good doctors

Sometimes the noodles had hamburger
most of the time they didn't
Out of habit, my sister waited
to go to the doctor
and now it's too late

Let's shut her down, boys!

    I see my mother standing
    in front of an open window
    It's summer
    She's wringing a dishtowel
    dry in her hand

Elmo Goes Emo

Elmo's soul is black as obsidian
Elmo's pain is only dampened by
the jagged cuts upon
Elmo's arms

Elmo made them with a beer bottle cap

Elmo wonders who can remember
the sun
Elmo's heart torn like crepe paper

The stain on Elmo cannot be washed away
Not even by *Tide*
and *Tide* knows fabric best

Wind. Frigid. Cold. Winter.

Snuffleupagus has a trunk like a baseball bat

Elmo shouldn't have said that

Elmo's going to be gutted like a rat

Tickle Elmo? Please
tickle Elmo

until Elmo can't breathe.

Sestina McRib

When god pulled that bow of bone
from Adam he couldn't have seen this
coming. Or maybe he could. They say he
sees everything coming. I don't.
At least not until it's too late.
And now the McRib

is back. Two dollars. It's not really a rib,
that's the fast one. This boneless
gift used to be sloppy, out of control. Lately
its act has come together. This
fist full of little problems. I don't
want to sound sentimental, but Ronald, he

must have wept, how he
must have wailed when the McRib
was torn from his side. Lonely doesn't
touch the lack of it. The missing bone
so long a part of his flesh. This,
you said, sauce on your hands, isn't real meat and later

that half-eaten sandwich tempts me. It's late,
you are asleep, I am drunk, he,
God, not Ronald, would deny me this.
I eat anyway, devour it, the McRib,
and the bone
bleached gaze of the moon doesn't

make me feel guilty at all. I do not
feel guilty at all. It's too late
for that. And of Adam, and his lost bone,
I wonder if he
missed it? Reached for it at night like the rib
was there only to find this:

                        this
empty pillow, this car full of empty wrappers. Don't
dwell on it much. Think of the McRib.

Even now when it is getting late,
try not to think of the way he
must have felt, a sack of meat and missing bones.

I saw this coming too late.

Don't let its lack of bones fool you.
Everything is falling apart except the McRib.

BRETT UNDERWOOD

How Far Does the Head Turn?

The hawk's shadow is motionless
high in the limbs
against a winter haze
above the alley as he peers
off the back porch
inhaling the ghosts of friends
some of them dead
through the filter

11 p.m.

He is waiting for it to pounce
and wonders if it is instead an owl
as the neighbor
to the East lets his
hounds out
and then back in
when the beast with wheels
to support crippled hind-quarters
yelps

Silence returns
as he gazes at faint Christmas Eve stars
and sips the last of the Imperial Stout

a gift
wondering how the urban bird's vision
differs from his

Bones aching from the clench of
the steering wheel
along winding roads
mind easing from the
white
line
fever
caught from the country hills reunion
and the stress of the holiday week

He is only sure that he is
where he is

Innards wrestle with the dichotomy
of lost childhood idiocy
and a huge meal
while his head swims in thoughts
of a dead father and the quote
his mother included on the
card
from Hafiz
something about God's yearning for
the playfulness in your eyes

The sluggish impulse to denounce
tradition

and hopes that he is choosing
the correct path
in delicious cocktails
complete the dilemma

South St. Louis dreams
as the head swivels and
the eyes shine

Day

In silence after vultures bickered over
the dead armadillo,
He rose and yearned, slurped and
put on the sky inside out
squinched his nose
donned his shoes stuffed his
mitts in his hip pockets
snot nosed and weary sensing
a bunch of sumac and sassafras
listening for a distant cry of
a wasp or whippoorwill
a crane, a bird of any other
kind
even a train whistle,
or the light of a star.

When finally came the faint whisper,
with a twist of his fingers on the
knob
a voice on the radio
across the sleeping souls
and educated pisswillies of doom
boiled in the urine of virgin boys.

Vicious gobs of phlegm
a damn leak in the engine roof
up a spider's ass halved
open with a torch

and after awhile
it went to sand
and they beat the dried leaves
of the lady's slipper into a powder.

Cackled and slapped his thigh
but missed the fly
used a mixture of chimney soot
and lard.

The old timer shut his trap,
accentuated with a solemn nod
and a puff of the stub of a
cigar

It ain't your Friday yet, Boy.

Slick

The bird of paradise knows no
no-fly zone and there is no potion
too potent to the surrealist;
thus profit the hunter and the pusher.
Still, Uncle Dave's convinced he's got a
shot with the wet nurse and her soapy
strokes until she slows the drip.
The strap of any purse won't
deny the carefree snatcher
oblivious to the ubiquitous cams
like a forearm shiver or a
slapstick banana peel
on a day when the plankton
are plentiful for the great fish
and the finned mammals while
the lefty lays one down the middle
to the tater king who whiffs on the next two
dipping junk balls and won't get action
from the starlets and doesn't care,
his dreams buried in the depths of the mitt
and his shrunken nuts.
When the wet blades give to the swift
sickle of the harvester who lost his
lumbago in the grace of an efficient arc
the news networks are on picnic
their 12-point lines carrying the sweet
smell of clean sheets in the lilac breezes

that yearn to carry the laundress' perspiration
to the docks
where the slime of fornicating slipper snails
know no laws of friction,
just the inevitable death
at the bottom of the orgy
and the larger males
that take their place as females,
sequentially hermaphroditic and not
likely to inbreed and weather
Old Testament judgment only to
find their post-coital demise
despite shells and iron-deficient
waifs still squeamish about
texture slicker than a
finger in the honey.

JORDI ALONSO

[p. 42]

        I should
tell you the truth,

               the dark   I love:
   a grotto   among

              the woods,

                       when

                nymphs

                 understand

[p. 88]

                Pan

      had

       new flowers

                  in

                      his

          step

      where   nymphs

            sculpt

                      white bones

           to

                   marble

[pp. 228-229]

I

will

              bring home

the power

                as

            a

                    Faun

                            must

                to

                speak

                          terror

at the

wolf that

cannot

              repose

JEANETTE POWERS

Throw Yourself Down the Hill

When I was a child I relished rolling down the hill. Making yourself a sausage link with your hands gripping your thighs or each other above the head and being perpendicular to the plane of descent and just letting gravity do her work, while you turned on your inner axis and bumped and bounced your way down to the place the ground plateaus. This was the summer equivalent to sledding, the dry slide, the way you passed your time in the heat of an afternoon. Sometimes I kept my eyes closed, but sometimes, I kept them open: Green Blue Green Blue Green Blue.

I've become fixated on throwing myself in the river and letting her take me rolling down all those ripples down to wherever she'd let me back out. Which, less melodramatically, would be wherever I left my car down river. So, Mateo comes to visit and off we go in two cars down to 3rd Creek where there's a half-assed drop in point, brought to you be the MO Conservation Department, at the spot 3rd Creek and the Gasconade meet. There's also a deep, deep hole there with a swing on the sandy beach for running and dropping into the water.

We leave the maroon four-door with a bottle of tequila and a joint and head back in my CRV to the house, walk the mile past the horse, the corral, through the cow pasture, past the dream house, down the fire road through the selfie stone meadow, and into Rocklayer Creek. I take Mateo over the rocks and around the roses, which I've come to learn aren't that at all, but are green briar. Pesky all the same. We stay quiet to lose the dogs. This is a dog-free day. We take the creek all the way to the river, it's 9 am.

We wade out to the middle of the current, well away from turtle/snake's lair, and we look upstream. *I say hold my hand, and we are gonna just fall back into a dead man's float and let the river take us away.* I look with the deepest love at the distant rushing water coming at us. I imagine the Butterfly Girl telling me again about how the heart is a port on the great river of the universe. I remember telling her I've dug to the bottom of my heart and there I found a tremendous and miniscule wall which encases it, impassable. I know that I covet that wall in a way that I can't bring it down. My heart won't throw itself anywhere, my heart is a garrison hidden deep in a feral world. I seem wild, but at the core, I'm all locked up.

We fall, hand in hand. I keep my eyes open, green blue green blue green blue, the trees line the sky. I'm taken away. Mateo and I saw that along highway D from the Farm to 3rd Creek is 6 miles, so we are figuring six or seven miles to swim. We imagine the river clocks at maybe 2 knots, so 2 miles an hour for 6 miles and high noon at the rope swing is our plan.

I'm thrown headlong into my river. There's nothing but being moved, allowing myself to be moved. Relinquishing all the standing against, and just going along. I am where the mountains meet the lowest part of the land, I am where the water table emerges, I am in the space of the runoff of storms, I am surging alongside, headed back to where I came from, the ocean. Salty womb of my being, my ultimate destination on this journey (which is the Mediterranean, but I won't get there for another month). I'm an excellent floater, I've often said *I'd never drown* because I can paddle water for days, I can dead man's float for years. There's some things growing up poor is good for: stamina is one.

I think about Sisyphus again, how if he loved pushing the rock and he loved being thrown down his hill, his life would be complete. We think of purpose. His purpose is to push the rock up, so he's robbed when it rolls away. Maybe his purpose is to keep things rolling, which means he has to get that rock back up from the low place of the river and the water table. Maybe the walls around my heart will get holes in them from Butterfly Girl's river, maybe one day the walls will fall apart with gravity and sink down to the river bottom, be someone else's special rock, and I will be ocean bound, finally.

Mateo is a rare bird. Crossdressing-sad-clown and super-genius-total-failure. He'd be Andy Warhol's muse, he'd outdrink Bukowski, he's a classic bad luck story wrapped up in a trust fund kid who spent all his money on books and drugs. He's the only one I know who would blindly throw himself down the river with me without a single hesitation and without conjecturing about how the day would go. He's *is* as is can be. Also, he can't float like me, so he's belly down and chin up in the knee-deep water, using his lanky arms to pull himself along while his legs flow out behind him. He has a white blonde Mohawk and blue eyes. He laughs a lot and thinks complaining is cute.

He has a beer in his hand which he's drinking and two more in the pockets of his swim trunks. He doesn't think of things like snacks or towels or maps or what if I break a bone or water to drink under the growing heat of the day. He just swims along cracking fart jokes and lightly gossiping and telling me forever how I'm the brightest star in his sky. Once he told me that I was like *the last seat in a helicopter heading out of Vietnam.* Everyone should have the pleasure of being loved by a Mateo in their lives. His mouth is a river, an ongoing rush of invention and giggles, the portal of his story-filled head.

I say *shhhhhhhhhhhhh.* He looks at me wounded, my smile sends sooth. I point above, a bald eagle is riding thermals. His eyes rise up and I shush him again, knowing already he's going to shout out with joy at seeing this. His tall frame stops himself in the river and I stop with him. We hold our ground against the pressure of the current and watch the eagle flying towards us along the water line, his mate joins him, crisscrossing the river until both of them disappear into the tree line.

Mateo leaps up with a Whitmanian *yawp*. We've arrived. His forever verbal patter takes a new tone now. He slows down. He's found river time, now. I can see it overtake him, as the city washes away and the fervor subsides and he can just be thrown down the river without having to fill in every blank space. I see he is seeing the slivers in the blank spaces he never noticed before.

Things are moving along at just the right speed: the speed they go at. Mateo polishes off the first beer and crushes it back into his pocket, then cracks the second and we float. Easy, laughing and quiet, the water is sometimes deep and sometimes very shallow, the mountain of the farm is tall on our right, rock catapults up and shows the life story of the river over so many years. It's all plateau on our left, some houses emerge and fade, sometimes a boat comes roaring from one way or the other, it's a holiday weekend.

At some point in the first hour, nature *calls*. Well, shit. I didn't bring any toilet paper. Well, shit. How does one shit on the river? This is a first. For me, anyway. There's a bit of a creek peeking about on the left and a fallen tree just about toilet seat high. I wade out of the water and head over. I'm just gonna sit way back on this sitting tree and poop over the back edge onto the sandy beach, then get back in the water and treat the river momentarily like a bidet. Mateo watches me drop my bikini bottom and hollers out the obvious question: *what are you doing?*

I'm pooping! I take one wary look back into my improvised bowl. There's a huge beautiful snail there, but time is of the essence and I complete my task. I holler back at Mateo, *I'm pooping on a snail!* Because he loves everything base and butt related. He squeals with delight and informs me that in the Ozarks, this is a sure-fire sign of impending disaster: the broken mirror, the black cat, the dead albatross, the shat upon snail. Also, he decides, I can't be the only pooping one.

At this point we are in a deep spot and I finish and swim back over to where he is treading water. He cheers my defecation with last of the second beer and crushes it into his pocket, retrieving the last. He sets the full beer afloat into the current where it bobs with the ripples. Of course, I can't be the only one pooping he tells me, but he is going to poop directly into the river to see if the poop floats like the full beer can and like me. He takes his swim trunks off and delights that they float alongside us, too! Mateo decides we need a Spanish Armada, a flotilla of many floating things to journey with us to 3rd Creek and grabs a nearby lost fence gate he calls *Fencie*, three sticks and a huge log he calls *Logodger*.

It's at this point he realizes that the swim trunks don't float after all. His britches are nowhere to be found. We struggle up stream in the deep water back to where maybe we saw the blue plaid trunks before. No dice. It's the Curse of the Shat Upon Snail. Now Mateo is naked but for his river shoes.

We laugh, but I cannot stop with the laughing, this is the cost of throwing oneself down the hill, down the river, there's no turning back and you only have what you brought and can keep. He can't keep a thing, he's the punk rock Charlie Brown, kicking his own ass forever. The boats and houses keep meandering and rushing by and he has to throw his ass down into the shallow water every time because his is a flag no one salutes. His balls and ass are dragging along the rock bottom of the river bed and beginning to show signs of wear and tear after the next hour of swimming. We're using Fencie and Logodger as pool rafts and noodles. Mateo is straddling Logodger and I giggle every time I imagine his delicate taint being chaffed by the rough bark. Mateo is all smiles, too.

There are eagles and fish and deer and rock ledges and frogs and boats and giggles and sweet talks and hot dishes about what's going on back home and tormented dreams of impossible loves and stories of what we are working on and reading and ideas we want to dream about next year and distant caws of crows and vultures circling and nearly not a trace of anything a man has built. This is the cathedral of the river and the power water has to make its own way.

We're expecting high noon to bring us to 3rd Creek and the rope swing and the tequila. As the sun reaches that apex, we are tired and I can feel the heat of a sunburn spreading across my face from the reflection on the water. Mateo has searched in vain for some sort of covering for his "utensil", but he doesn't fit into a single one of the abandoned tires on the river's edge. *They're too big in the wrong places and too small in the wrong places,* he whines delightedly. We giggle. Finally, as we lament that each turn doesn't turn up our drop out point, he looks to me and asks the question I've been dreading: *Did you look at a map, ever?*

No.

So, you don't even really know that 3rd Creek dumps into the Gasconade?

No. But I'm really, really confident it does.

It's this point I know why a Mateo is better than any ten thousand other poets or folks, he is an undaunted explorer, he shrugs and goes forward. He knows how to commit to throwing oneself down the hill. We begin an assay into rock climbing; well, I should say I do. He stays behind with the river acting as his pants. I forage up deer trails and rocky inclines testing house after house to find someone to help us. We're lost, we're tired, we're hungry, and he's naked.

I laugh.

No one's home, probably due to the holiday, we keep onward. Mateo finds the remnants of a burlap sack in some dead brush. It's just wide enough to go from hip bone to tip of his dick. It's just long enough to wrap around his waist and be tied. It also ties around the base of his ass, but is definitely leaving both cheeks exposed to the breeze. He finds another cord of burlap and uses it to tie from front to back making a sort of Ozarkian Sumo Diaper. This gives him an inordinate amount of confidence. He puffs big and strong like he's ready for a bout. I am an infinity of giggles.

Finally, we see two boats we've seen pass us a couple times tied to a dock. Here is our ticket out. We climb the rocks and just as we are about to hoist ourselves up the hill to their house, another boat sees us. Mateo jumps back into the river to hide his diaper.

I raise a hand and the motor quells, I holler out: *We're lost!*

What are ya'll doin?

We were gonna swim from the Farm to 3rd Creek, but now we're lost.

Well, hell, that's 6 more miles down the river! You're swimming? Ya'll got no innertube? No nothing?

No.

You're grounded! You both are grounded! Come on and climb in, I'll take ya down there.

At this point Mateo raises his hand from the river.

There's just one more thing ... I'm naked.

Aren't we all, Mateo? Just some of us more obviously than others.

VICTOR CLEVENGER

a poem about a woman i never got to know

it disgusts her   she once said
everything from the rough slaughter
to the hot sizzle

feathers floating on a
wretched breeze

grease smeared on lips
rubbin' bones

just thinking about it   she told me
that she could almost vomit
right now   but she didn't

she looked like winona ryder
dark hair & cute

she ordered a glass of ice water
with a lemon   asked for a cucumber
slice as well

& i'm not sure
where she is these days

& i really don't give a damn either

she's crazy   & hates fried chicken

there aren't many good men i know
who have time for a woman
like that

we stand next to a river

i take a drag from my cigarette   slip my shoes off
take another drink of high life & sit the can down in
the sand   take my shirt off   hang it on a
branch   take my pants off & hang them next
to my shirt   my underwear are blue

i watch her strip her clothes off & hang them near
mine   her underwear are pink & black

the sun is white   hot   & beating down on our
pale freckled shoulders

holding hands   we walk down the bank towards
the edge of a small cliff like two kids in a cheap
slasher film

not at all concerned about the tales of catfish
big enough to swallow men   lying naked in mud
& muck   wearing the slimy coats
of a thousand unfulfilled dreams that have been
cast out with lead sinkers for generations

we jump   shouting with excitement
hands thrown above our heads waving
free-falling without a care

& i wish that love these days
could make me feel
that way again

when

a star strangled sky rumbles
it brings back memories
of a summer night

twenty-five years ago

when we crawled on the ground
searching for a lost five-dollar bill
by the short casted shine
of a cigarette lighter's flame

it's gone for sure   she said

just before i leaned in
& tried to kiss her for the first time
behind a dying forsythia bush
that i was certain could keep the secret

that there was never even
a five-dollar bill
to begin with

KEVIN W. PEERY

Rosie

I grew up watchin'
the Jetsons
and always thought
by the time I turned thirty
I might have a Rosie
of my own

At the end of every day
she would meet me
at the door
with an ice cold
Hendrick's Buck
and freshly-lit
Five Star cigar

Later in the evenin'
Rosie might play
a medley of
Bob Seger songs
while grillin' my steak
and askin' me
about my day

Unfortunately this is not
the way things panned out...

Goddamned Hanna-Barbera

Guess I'll have to start
watchin' reruns
of the Jefferson's
and try to find
a place in my heart
for a Florence instead

Cecil

Cecil Smith
sold me
a Chinese Rolex
after church
last Sunday

He said it
was the last one
he would have
for a while
since the Feds
are really watchin' him

This suspect Submariner
ain't too shabby
for just a shade over a C-Note

In fact...
I'll probably only wear it
on special occasions

Like to the
Evel Knievel
Thrill Show
out in Topeka
or over to
Jeff City
where I'll visit
ole Cecil...in prison again

Shaver

The first time
I met Billy Joe Shaver
we shot the shit
in the Retro Lounge
at Knuckleheads Saloon

This was a few years
prior to Pastor Carl
converting the
space into his
Gospel Lounge

Shaver said the
room reminded him
of a feed store
off China Spring road
down in Waco

It had a few
second hand seats...
with an old art deco couch
that was situated under
an etching of
Shotgun Willie Nelson

I just sat there silent
while Billy Joe

told a story about
the time he drove
his chopper up on
Harlan Howard's
front porch in Nashville

He said he wished like hell
someone woulda told him
how big ole Harlan was...

I was thinkin' to myself
Damn you Shaver...

I wish somebody
woulda told me
ten years ago
that you were
the greatest
I'd a drove
my ole
ragged ass truck
down to Waco
just to try -n-
catch a glimpse

CHIGGER MATTHEWS

Working On My Car

Somewhere I think to myself
it is Wednesday
and what's more humbling than that?
A razor the size of a rabbit's tooth
falcon feet.
Fact is you're not here
and hay bales golden buck teeth
      of ol' time romancers are distant memories
      of faded glory.
This is to say nothing about the Department of
Transportation,
      the Army Corps of Engineers, or
      local law enforcement
in the summer.
Flowers bloom where they are.
I think this is beautiful while I change a flat tire:
how art is idle,
a kind of heavy air
about as useful as a cold beer
      to an already drunk baby and how
it is Wednesday.

Optimism and Confidence

On the road this poetry conquers and consumes
rawhide
razorback
city-slickin'
riverbilly
northward ho!
On the static banks of the Gasconade River
red quinoa crawls with ants
somehow semiotically related to
masturbation which is interesting in
light of Lincoln's famous words,
I would rather watch a man fight bees
and I have to agree,
it beats watching a man defend himself from
ants in pants.

Memory

No birdsong is as beautiful as your human voice
and truth is, I wish you'd shut the fuck up.
Echos and mirrors over a
vaulted ceiling channel two
abysses staring into electric introspective
jack-in-a-box
        with a fox
                wearing socks
recalling childhood ambitions
horizons and steel-beams or else
        green canopies will turn
                brown in the Fall
                        become gray and
                              die while yet living.
I see now that
this is another poem
about a road.

HUNTER PENDER

I Could Write You into a Soft Evening

I could write you into a soft evening,
making you the glow of a sunset reaching across a
million trees; the sky so pink the moon hides half his
face from her blushing.

Still sea foam green water rippling from pebbles trying
to be skipped.
Wind chimes playing the quietest song as you move your
fingertips across your lovers back.
Summer drunk goodnights when the sheets are cool
after a bath.

I could write you into a stormy morning,
making you the clank of a flag hitting against a pole.
The sun hiding behind
dark
dark
clouds
and only lightning illuminating an empty basement full
of bad memories in the back of your mind.
The temperature dropping too quickly and the electric is
out.

I could write you into a different body:
phantom hands and a phantom heart,
but everything would most likely be dead because I do
not know how to let go of ghosts.

The truth is, baby,
you only taught me one word in your language:
Paani.
You told me it meant water.
And I am so goddamn hung up on that.
Water.
Water surrounds the home I live in, so do you surround
the home I live in?
Perhaps it is me.
Perhaps I am flowing like water, touching you and Asia
at the same time

Did it Hurt?

Did it hurt?
Lucifer,
did it hurt being cast out of the only home you ever knew?

Imagine the dizziness Satan must have known when he stood
at the edge of heaven, looking down at humanity:
the only evidence that God could be defeated.

Imagine how he felt hurling past dust and comets:
wind rushing through his ears and his beautiful,
beautiful
face,
becoming colder as each one of his wings ripped off and used
as constellations.

The devil did not become the devil when he became woke.
He became the devil halfway through his fall as he watched
reality become closer and illusion grow smaller and smaller
behind him.

The love he had for his father was replaced with bitterness.
Hatred was pushed into his soul where compassion should be.
Every child who has been abandoned by his parents has felt
what the devil felt in that moment.

We know this story.
We do not have to think before speaking it.

This feeling of sudden aloneness.
The moment our consciousness is thrown into existence.

Why are we here?
What are we doing?
Why is everybody looking down?

This feeling has been passed down from generations.
We ignore that Satan was God's favorite angel and go straight to the part when he is falling from the clouds.
He must have lit up the sky with his demise.
He must have shined so brightly that surely Eve wrote love songs about the sun never comparing to the white hot flame of lucifer.
And Adam was jealous but oh there was no better way to turn our attention to the sky for the first time.

The sky is bright tonight. The sky is bleeding hearts of strangers tonight. So it goes that new love comes with new hands that desperately try to erase past fingerprints.

Write Me on Waves

Write me on waves so I mean everything in one moment and nothing in the next:
I only want you,
I want everything you have.

Write me into the clouds and wait for a storm to kiss the ground and bounce back:
I'll come back for you,
I'll be better in the fall.

Write me in smoke so by the time you put out your cigarette you will have forgotten you thought about me at all:
I have all of this love inside of me,
but I am no longer soft.

Write me into the Winter and tell me you hate snow:
I always melt for you ...

I am so naked and singular. Haven't you realized that?

JIM MCGOWIN

Unum

I could be red cruelty,
the wound which refuses to heal,
a mouth
that stitches conversations into silence.

I am bound mad within the wound
and the word —
to cease is to exist within
the abundance of death in meaning.

One face to live, to write from,
one face to drink from Lethe.

What fear? What hush?
What sound? What dream?

I hide in my own marrow,
in the marrow of these marginal proposals
which are my own entanglement,
my sustenance and ruse.

Devised in a violation of self,
and crowning through their discomfort.

Damned to writhe in linguistic mirages —
to choke in grand atmospheres,
to respire through
an accumulation of drowning impediments,

Seeking shelter within labyrinthine architecture,
only to deconstruct in blind excavation,
in order to cancel out the rigor mortis of shape.

An emotion is called black because of the color,
but what of the color of crows?
Do they receive such scrutiny
because of what they appear to be on the outside?
Little dabs of metaphors in a green field,
merely seeking to estimate
the necessity of enduring loss from interrogation?
No one can cut cleaner edges,
given only blunt scissors for wings.

The words are changed into wild machines,
interconnected by pipes that pump
the blood of the dead,
the language and power of the dead,
the fearlessness contained
in their paralyzed tongues.

Condensation of brilliance and lunacy,
a duplicity of madness carved out in opaque sigils,
eroding inert language with a law of silence.

No one brushes the sky
like a perfectly written black bird,
splashed in ink spread,
complete in divine velocity,
its wilderness voice
beyond the abstract barriers of
inarticulate hesitation.

I opened a breach in the twilight
with my eye,
like a sun,
full of blind love
that seeks every color
reflected from both sides of the restless flutter.

A burdened mechanical existence,
built to dissect implications
seen cowering in the voluminous cracks
between every word on the already
decaying pages.

I must apologize — it was very cruel of me
to disguise myself as a poem.

As punishment,
let me go blind from the allure,
the eyes—
drinking up fountains of bitterness and adaptation
in order to redefine focus as clarity,
to exchange direction for doldrums.

My silence is in-between,
it is the changeling state of the word,
the disappearance of cohesive language,
born in the afterbirth and ashes of the hunt.

Collect this blood, my own *Asperges,*
splash it and hold it accountable
for the strange feathering designs
it makes on the floor
in attempted explanation,
before it trickles to the gutters.

A reasonable solution
to quell a large breach in a rotting beast,
eternally perched on the edge
ready to cannibalize its next oeuvre heart.

Because it is
as I have always suspected —

I am the horizon
for which Death seeks
in vehement sweeps of the sky,

Measured out
one pretty little sentence
at a time.

Antigone

Determined
to die,
by action of birthing
us
into the dark,

Who can hold their lips
closed in asylum?

Who creates the hands
that would allow their own rope
to go taut?

She,
who breaths upwards
only to keep the birds aloft,

To witness the city's
most arrogant architectures.

Sure will be her children.

Sure will be her children,
who hold no manufactured gods
in the agony of their solitude,

Sure will be her children,
who need no violence of apologies,

Sure will be her children
in their asphyxiated dreaming,

Held in breath,

Held in resolve,

Held in a loop of boundary
eternally tied,

Tired but unyielding,
like the weeping
eye of a noose.

Sigma Octanis

Starlight at the poles
explains the dissolution of a shadow
far better than any cultish doodle.

And as for opinions
regarding the horizon's subcontext,
one is as unnecessary as any,
assuming the astronomical evidence
is as baseless
as the acceptance of the temporary
is easy.

The northern and southern spirits
dance in circles,
rising beyond the comedy
of swift arrows and
slow targets,

But the interior is protected
against the darkness
of its own duplicity,
a Sigma Octanis to follow,
avoiding the ancestral alchemy
that changes elements of worth
into common ash and stone.

Ignorance of choice
is a remarkable character flaw.
What sort of evolutionary hoax
would differentiate a soul
from cold brown clay?

A hollow disposition
written in broken mirror complicity,
and a failure to accept
that there can be no other stars
left to confuse,

Those who walk backwards
while searching the sky
for a way in.

"Nobody Lives Here Anymore," Justin Hamm

JOHN DORSEY

Nikki, Full of Grace
for Steve Goldberg and Bob Phillips

the first time we ever met
you wore sunglasses
in the basement
of a south toledo punk club
where i was reading poetry
in the dark

backed up by a strung out piano player
under a photo of g.g. allin

bob went out to his car
& came back
with a half used jesus candle
from the dollar store

that lit up the room

with an outline of your face
thin like a wafer

like the bones
of a half written patti smith song
about the madonna's last days
spent counting the stars
over detroit

the fire in your eyes
burning the fingers of anyone
who dared to touch you.

The Midwestern Guide to Time Travel

remember to dance in a 10 ft. steel cage
one for every year of your life

to dream of a future
filled with flying cars
and international date lines
that seem as limitless
as homespun wisdom

somewhere a little voice
tells you to drown a mermaid
in 39 ft of water or a hill of dirt

it sings for blood
as the sun
touches your skin.

Moon Over Eufaula, Oklahoma
for Victor Clevenger

just south of muskogee
dumpster cats guard crumbling pyramids
& discarded bbq grills
in the moonlight

the creek nation girls still dance
in honor of their own virginity
covered in dust
& humble bones
yelling free bird lives

free bird lives

here everyone is loyal
& your breath just hangs there
as heavy as a cloud

& apartments are shaped
like tombstones

& the outline of a girl's hips
in the shadow of a lonely gas station
can still transport you back
to a better time.

JUSTIN HAMM

Arthur and Marie, 1961

Late autumn now, Illinois. The trees, half-dead,
wave their gnarled arms above the bone
white gravel of the rural country road

down which he steers the old rustbucket flatbed,
her nose toward the pinkish twilight, toward a town
where they'll meet his folks for supper.

The day has been a long one, full of harsh fieldwork
and minor disagreements that kept them from sharing
they've both been dreaming of a child again.

Now he is sorry and she is ready to let him be,
and so his hand bridges their space, finding her cheek
for a sweet second before shooting back to the wheel.

At the far reach of their headlights, a great ghostlike bird—
a snowy owl, perhaps, though rare around here.
It sits in stony stillness between the drying cornfields.

Consider the intricacies of human recollection.
If she is, in fact, with child, they will one day turn
this vision into an omen, even making an angel

of its wide white wings and its sudden skyward ascension,
everything electric with importance—their shallow breath
as they watch, eyes wide and unblinking, the way

their hands find each other and interlock on her knee.
Just as true is the opposite—the bird becomes the angel
of death if what's stirs in her is instead malignant.

But if she is empty, except for her basic dissatisfaction,
then the vision astonishes only for that brief instant.
Once it is gone, it is, truly and finally, gone.

In fact, trees, road, twilight, autumn, corn: all gone,
the whole scene blended into the dense camouflage
of memory, forgotten fifteen years, then twenty more,

until even that cells-deep desire for a child of their flesh
is lost to them, buried beneath her kindly cynicism,
barred behind his stoic, even-if-my-back's-broke will.

Forgotten so long it is left, finally, to the storyteller's invention.
Buried so deep when the dust is finally blown off
they can only imagine it a fiction that never existed at all.

First Lesson in Vietnam, 1987

It was how you stood on your trailer roof
all that sweltering Independence Day, caped
in a threadbare flag of our nation, encircled
by Budweiser empties, plates of burning incense.
It was how you stood there and also how,
lit from above by those colorful celebration
bombs, you made me believe in the myth
of the romantic savage. I had no idea then
what you'd tried to accomplish alone
in the toolshed with the extension cord,
nor how, in a few years, you'd be hauled in—
armed robbery, just days after the first
Gulf War broke out. I saw only your hair,
shoulder length, and your scarred torso
bare and bony, home to a tattooed menagerie
of fantasy creatures: elf, dragon, phoenix,
centaur, faerie, citizens of a land
to which you'd gladly defect. It was all that,
and it was how recklessly you lit
bottle rockets and fired them from your
hollowed-out walking stick. And it was how—
finally—when my father cupped his hands together
and shouted, Hey, Chuck, give it a rest, guy.
It's getting pretty late, you turned, delicate
as a dancer in the shimmering moonlight,
and offered him what little was left
of your mangled middle finger.

Pay Phones in the Underworld

My best friend texts me
a picture of a letter my mother
sent him the year she died.
He had forgotten about it
and wants to know whether
I want it for myself?

But the power isn't so much
in the ownership.
It arises from the surprise
in seeing the long loops
of her letters unexpectedly,
how they seem to carry
the very sound of her voice.

The dead know these things.
At just the right moment
they leave off from doing
their secret dead doings
and find a payphone, fish around
for change deep in the pockets
of their burials suits.

The call comes through
and on this end I pass a Camaro
just like the one Mom
rose hell with when we were kids.

Or the V.C. Andrews novels
stacked at the community yard sale
resurrect in my mind the rhythm
of her breathing as she read
evenings by yellow lamplight
in our smoky trailer.

But it's no use calling them.
The dead almost never answer.
You only tie up the line
as they stand patiently by,
tapping bony fingers to skulls
and waiting for the ringing to stop
so they know for certain the need
for reminder has ripened.

WILLIAM TROWBRIDGE

To the Cialis Lovers

What mortals or gods are these? O attic shape!
Fair attitude! With breed of bathtub-seated man
and maiden near-o'erwrought among a span
of oaks or near the ocean. Bold lovers, napes
and thighs are out; but holding hands may reap
some hay. Cold pastoral with separate ceramics
warmed by ardor and Tadalafil, tidy as Saran,
set to sail the Merlot-dark sea or L.L. Beanscape.

When old age hath this generation blurred,
you — or your replacements — shall still beard woe
and its gloomy offspring. O friend of humankind
to whom you say, *Beauty's for the birds,*
and Truth has toodled south not far behind —
that's all we know on earth or care to know.

Head Out on the Highway

We were Grand Canyon bound from Omaha,
1200 miles of mostly two-lane, the '50s kind
with curbs that sucked you onto the shoulder.

July and no AC, my sister and I bored
into sparring over gum and comic books,
Dad firing up his slow burn as Mother

pointed out the sights—sage brush,
cacti, mountains, cacti, sage brush—
and we kids shrieked for *tourist attractions,*

which boasted alligators, two-headed snakes,
Aztec mummies, jackalopes. When darkness
came, we'd stop at the Come On Inn,

or the Gorilla Villa, where I'd waste
a quarter on the not-so-Magic Fingers,
semis blasting by, rattling the windows.

Dad watching a toilet overflow or TV
fizzle, declared this was as close to hell
as he'd ever been. And he was in the War.

Twenty miles from Flagstaff, he hit
overload and blew, said he'd turn back
if he heard another yap—not the classic

empty threat, we found at next yap,
when our travel film jerked into reverse
and reeled us to our flatland home.

The Crazy Lady

She was crazy. Why else the wild,
white hair, dislike of children,
and yard-full of ornaments: elves,

trolls, glass balls, wizards, toads?
Her house, just outside the two-block
boundary our parents set for us,

could make a sunny afternoon
grow sinister. We pedaled our bikes
at top speed when we passed by,

skipped it on Halloween, when —
we knew—her kind could tempt
boys and girls inside and shrink

them down for planting in her
window box. At night one Fourth
of July we tossed a jumbo string

of Black Cats in her yard. Another
night, we slipped onto her back porch
and peeked through a window.

An ancient broom, of course, leaned
ready by the door. When she heard
our fumblings, she rose from her chair,

yelled after us in Witch as we ran
home. We got our first close look
at her the day an ambulance

pulled up and loaded her inside.
She looked worn out, ancient,
too fragile to do harm. We watched

as the ambulance eased away
and disappeared in traffic,
knowing we couldn't get so old.

"Spinner," Greg Edmondson, pencil and gouache on pattern maker's paper, 42"x42," 2013

Jordi Alonso graduated with an AB in English from Kenyon College in 2014 and was the first Turner Fellow in Poetry at Stony Brook University where he received his MFA. He is a Gus T. Ridgel Fellow in English at the University of Missouri where he is a PhD candidate studying the cultural transmission of nymphs and fauns in literature. He's been published in *Kenyon Review Online, Noble/Gas Qtrly, Luna Luna Magazine, Levure Littéraire,* and other journals. *Honeyvoiced,* his first book, was published by XOXOX Press in 2014, and his chapbook, *The Lovers' Phrasebook,* was published by Red Flag Poetry Press in 2017. He is an editor at Sundress Publications.

Steven H. Bridgens: Born: Kansas City, Missouri, Planet Earth, 1949, the year of the first Soviet nuclear test. Parents: healers, one trod the dark path and one the light. Siblings: one of each, both younger, iconoclasts and artists. Progeny: one son, a man now with his own trajectory and dreams. Current Fascinations: words, painting, sculpture, the ancient world or the idea of it, particularly the rebuilding of it, silence and the absence of it, sleep and the same, dead bluesmen, ancient Asian poets, the demi-monde, espionage, imagined, not real, the primeval forest of Buddhism in all its humble glory, the savage comic tyranny of the political stage, the toxic and liberating proscenium of the internet, the dark Jungian depths of the self, the flickering colored shadows of the cinema and architecture, the utopian possibilities of life on garden earth with our liberated sentient friends. Death: certain as to its eventuality but uncertain as to its time. Indifferent, but not unconcerned.

Victor Clevenger is a writer and poet who spends his days in a Madhouse and his nights with his second ex-wife, together they raise six children in a small town northeast of Kansas City, MO. Selected pieces of his work have appeared in a variety of places online and in print. His work has been nominated for the Best of the Net Anthology. His most recent collections of poetry include *Congenital Pipe Dreams* (Spartan Press, 2017), *Sandpaper Lovin'* (Crisis Chronicles Press, 2017) and *tom farris is my brother* (CWP Collective Press, 2017).

Daniel Crocker's work has appeared in *The Los Angeles Review, Hobart, Big Muddy, New World Writing, Stirring, Juked, The Chiron Review, The Mas Tequila Review* and over 100 others. His books include *Like a Fish* (full length) and *The One Where I Ruin Your Childhood* (e-chap with thousands of downloads) both from Sundress Publications. Green Bean Press published serveral of his books in the '90s and early 2000s. These include *People Everyday and Other Poems, Long Live the 2 of Spades*, the novel *The Cornstalk Man* and the short story collection *Do Not Look Directly Into Me*. He has also published several chapbooks through various presses. His newest full length collection of poetry, *Shit House Rat*, will be available from Spartan Press in September. He is the editor of *The Cape Rock* (Southeast Missouri State University) and the co-editor of *Trailer Park Quarterly*. He's also the host of the podcast, Sanesplaining, about poetry, mental illness and nerd stuff.

John Dorsey lived for many years in Toledo, Ohio. He is the author of several collections of poetry, including *Teaching the Dead to Sing: The Outlaw's Prayer* (Rose of Sharon Press, 2006), *Sodomy is a City in New Jersey* (American Mettle Books, 2010), *Appalachian Frankenstein* (GTK Press, 2015) and *Being the Fire* (Tangerine Press, 2016). He is the current Poet Laureate of Belle, MO. He may be reached at archerevans@yahoo.com.

Greg Edmondson was born in Durham, North Carolina. He earned his BFA from the University of Tennessee, Knoxville and MFA from Washington University in St. Louis. He is the recipient of numerous grants and awards including Fulbright and DAAD fellowships to Germany, and residency fellowships to Artpark, the Virginia Center for the Creative Arts and the Santa Fe Art Institute. He has shown widely throughout the United States and Europe and has works in collections both public and private. Currently Greg is an artist in residence at Osage Arts Community in Belle, Missouri.

Originally from the flatlands of central Illinois, **Justin Hamm** now lives near Twain territory in Missouri. He is the founding editor of *the museum of americana* and the author of *American Ephemeral* and *Lessons in Ruin,* as well as two poetry chapbooks. His poems, stories, photos, and reviews have appeared in *Nimrod, The Midwest Quarterly, Sugar House Review, Pittsburgh Poetry Review,* and a host of other publications. Recent work has also been selected for *New Poetry from the Midwest* (2014, New American Press) and the Stanley Hanks Memorial Poetry Prize from the St. Louis Poetry Center.

Chigger Matthews is currently a poet and writer in residence at the Osage Arts Community, just outside Belle, MO.

Raphael Maurice is a poet, translator, and teacher. He resides in Washington, MO where the river keeps its secrets.

Jim McGowin has a background in media communications and visual art. He prefers to write, paint and take photos when he isn't stuck at his day job. He has performed at various legitimate and nefarious reading series around Missouri, on St. Louis KDHX radio, and has written several chapbooks. He has spent some time rambling around Mexico but currently resides with his family in St. Louis MO.

Americana songwriter and Kansas City based poet, **K.W. Peery,** is the author of *Tales of a Receding Hairline, Purgatory, Wicked Rhythm and Ozark Howler.*
Tales of a Receding Hairline was a semifinalist in the Goodreads Choice Awards - Best in Poetry 2016. Peery is a regular contributor in *Veterans Voices* and the *Australia Times Poetry Magazine.* His work is included in the Vincent Van Gogh Anthology *Resurrection of a Sunflower* and the Walsall Poetry Society Anthology *Diverse Verse II.* Credited as a lyricist and producer, Peery's work appears on more than a dozen studio albums over the past decade.

Hunter Pender lives in Poplar Bluff, MO.

Jeanette Powers is an anarchist poet and performance artist. Her work centers around *desyncopation* and battling the cage of habit. She also focuses on intersectional community development, with an eye towards justice and equality. She currently helps build the performative arts venue Uptown Arts Bar, lit-fest Fountainverse, the three-year KC based monthly publishing sequence Pop Poetry, EMP Books independent press, and the arts non-profit Chameleon. She's authored six published books of poetry, and is working on her third "practice novel". Her newest book, *Gasconade* is released in April 2018 by NightBallet Press. She is a fellow-resident at Osage Arts Community and can most often be found running creeks with her hound dog, Olly Moss.

Jason Ryberg is the author of twelve books of poetry, six screenplays, a few short stories, a box full of folders, notebooks and scraps of paper that could one day be (loosely) construed as a novel, and, a couple of angry letters to various magazine and newspaper editors. He is currently an artist-in-residence at both The Prospero Institute of Disquieted P/o/e/t/i/c/s and the Osage Arts Community, and is an editor and designer at Spartan Books. His latest collections of poems are *Head Full of Boogeymen / Belly Full of Snakes* (Spartan Press, 2016) and *A Secret History of the Nighttime World* (39 West Press, 2017). He lives part-time in Kansas City with a rooster named Little Red and a billygoat named Giuseppe and part-time somewhere in the Ozarks, near the Gasconade River, where there are also many strange and wonderful woodland critters.

William Trowbridge's seventh poetry collection, *Vanishing Point*, was published by Red Hen Press in April, 2017. His graphic chapbook, *Oldguy: Superhero*, came out from Red Hen in 2016. His other collections are *Put This On, Please: New and Selected Poems*, *Ship of Fool*, *The Complete Book of Kong*, *Flickers*, *O Paradise*, and *Enter Dark Stranger*. He is a faculty mentor in the University of Nebraska Omaha Low-residency MFA in Writing Program and was Poet Laureate of Missouri from 2012 to 2016. For more information, see his website at wiliamtrowbridge.net.

Brett Lars Underwood writes near a confused Ficus plant in St. Louis. His influences and meter vary. Think of free jazz, the sex calls from early-morning birds or jackhammers outside the bedroom window. His verse and riddles have been published by *The Bicycle Review*, *52Nd City*, *The Subterranean*, *Bad Shoe*, *Ucityreview.com* and included in *Flood Stage: An Anthology of Saint Louis Poets*. He unleashed *Sunlit Insult*, his first chapbook, in 2011 and *Its Bush Lent Subtle Hints* hit the streets in October, 2013. His next book will be published by Spartan Press in 2018.

Steve Vogt is the mayor of Belle, MO

Brock

My son is gone,
He has left me so alone.
This has made me very sad,
What did he do that was so bad?

Why was he taken?
Left to wonder and be forsaken.
So young and so kind.
Others not so worthy left behind.

Is it not for me to question,
Am I being taught some kind of lesson?
Where to find the strength to keep trying,
I wake up and find myself crying.

Surely, I will see him someday,
My love for him will last forever anyway.
All I could do is watch him die,
Sadly, I didn't really get a chance to say goodbye.

—Steve Vogt

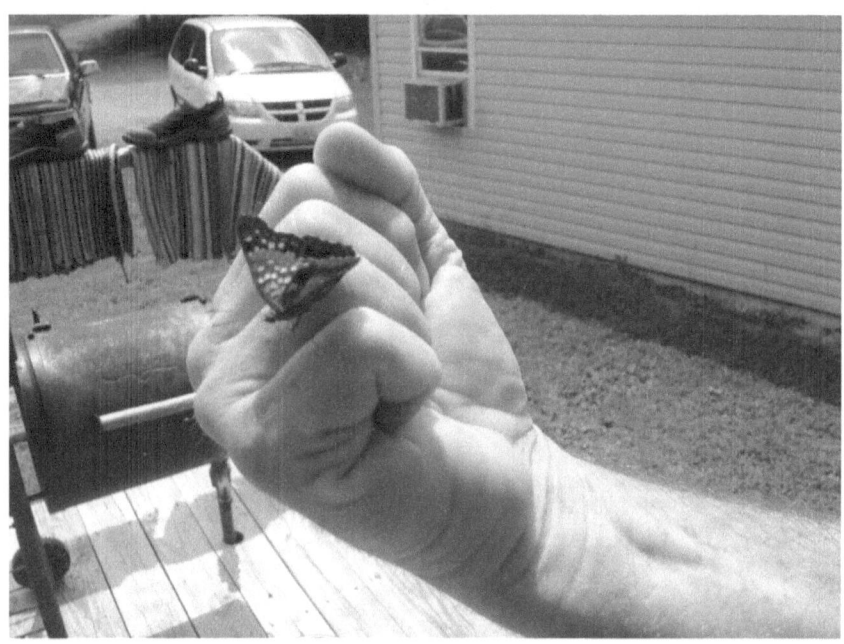

"Butterfly and Fist," Jason Ryberg

This project was made possible, in part, by generous support from the Osage Arts Community.

Osage Arts Community provides temporary time, space and support for the creation of new artistic works in a retreat format, serving creative people of all kinds — visual artists, composers, poets, fiction and nonfiction writers. Located on a 152-acre farm in an isolated rural mountainside setting in Central Missouri and bordered by ¾ of a mile of the Gasconade River, OAC provides residencies to those working alone, as well as welcoming collaborative teams, offering living space and workspace in a country environment to emerging and mid-career artists. For more information, visit us at www.oac.com

www.ingramcontent.com/pod-product-compliance
Lightning Source LLC
Chambersburg PA
CBHW021443080526
44588CB00009B/671